Accelerate

Dr. Monique Rodgers, D.M.

Accelerate

Dr. Monique Rodgers

DEDICATION

This book is dedicated to My mom Prophetess and Assistant Pastor Genise Rodgers for teaching me to never give up in life and for teaching me to pray and live for God. I love you so much! To Chief Apostle Fredrick J. Harris and Lady Lakendra Harris for your training and mentorship. To Chief Apostle Ron Spears and Lady Laverne Spears thank you for your continued support and encouragement. To Apostle David R. Watkins and Lady Tonya Watkins thank you so much for your encouragement and prayers. To Apostle Bianca Lowry thank you so much for your mentorship woman of God it has helped me to leap forth into all that God has for me. To Charmaine Gibson and James Gibson thank you so much your encouragement and support I thank God for you and love you both. To Apostle Wayne Rogers thank you so much for believing in me and for praying for me. To Nakeisa Jackson thank you so much for helping to build me and your continued leadership and support. To Chanel E. Martin thank you so much for helping me to grow as a leader and to ascend into all that God has given me to do in writing. To Dr. Judith and Darin McAllister thank you so much for teaching me the power of intercessory prayer. To Dr. Yvonne Capehart thank you so much for your encouragement and support. To Apostle John Eckhardt thank you so much for your support. To Pastor Sonia Yanez thank you so much for continual support and prayers daily. To Apostle Marcus Murray thank you so much for the Listen Effect on Clubhouse you have blessed my life tremendously I thank God for you believing in my dream. To my mentees Dani, Eileen, Jessica, Brianna, and Christy thank you so much for entrusting me as your mentor and helping to see you soar into all that God has for you and more. To "Auntie Tab" Tabitha Goodner thank you so much for seeing my vision and supporting it. I thank God for you and The Butlers! You are a tremendous blessing to my life! To every person that I have ever met this book is for you to encourage you to accelerate and to move forward into all that God has given unto you to master and complete for Glory in this lifetime.

Table of Contents

Introduction

Can you remember the first time that you stepped foot on an airplane or in an airport? What was it like? How did you feel? Well, if you are like me, I can remember the first time that I received a ticket in my hands to fly that there was such an excitement and anticipation about the unknown of going somewhere that I had never been before. At the time that I traveled I had the inquisitive mind of a teenager and the heightened interest of learning all that I could about traveling. As I walked through security and went through TSA, I remember the excitement that I felt of traveling and meeting new people and seeing a country that I had never be to before and learning of a new culture and way of life. I remember scanning the area where I sat waiting for the plane and watching the different mannerisms and those that has traveled before and the ones that were new to traveling how cautious and they were, and they carried a different aura about them than most. They had a peace that was centered in their presence that indicated they had traveled before and that they knew they destinations would be coming soon as they waited. A few years later after I had flown to several countries and cities, I too had gained the same concept with traveling and flying that helped me to appreciate the why behind each time that I stepped on an airplane and how beautiful it was to capture each moment and to sit next to a window seat after all the rushing of getting through to the plane, boarding, finding a seat and then finally getting into the air to the destination. What also inspired me was the opportunity that I now had to meet and connect with several people from all over the world and to learn something special about and at the same time find ways that I could attribute and add value to their lives whether it was talking about business, shoes, stocks, lip gloss, children, church, favorite choir songs or writing it was an opportunity to ascend and to recollect on a moment that I would never see again. Acceleration works the same way in our lives. We often believe that we have so much time to dedicate and to wait for things to be completed only to find out that the time we have is ever so valuable and how we attend to it and make use of it is important to our destiny.

Chapter One

Have a Flight Plan

I remember at the age of 16 flying to Jamaica, for the first time, I had never been on an airplane before. And I remember sitting in my seat and looking out the window and smiling at the fact that something new was happening in my life that I had never experienced. Little did I know that I was getting ready to embark on one of the greatest journeys of my life. That would change the trajectory of my life forever. As I was flying that day. And as the plane was getting ready to pull off. And to ascend. I felt such a tugging in my belly, that I had never experienced before, except for being on a roller coaster, or going up in an elevator, but this feeling was different. There was a level of elevation, that says, when you ascend. You're going to continue to go higher will continue to go up.

So, I began to ascend on the airplane, as it went up. And as the plane was ascending. Before that, the flight crew told us everything that we needed to do before we took off. And that is what God does. He gives us everything that we need to know everything that we need to do everything that we need to prepare before we take off and do all that he has called us to do a ministry. It was my first day of going overseas. I had never been before, but I was excited and anticipating all that I would see hear and learn about as I was there. And I was so honored at the fact that this couple that I went with had asked me to come in that they were excited as well to bring me on my first journey of what I would experience to be my first international travel of many.

As I flew on that airplane that day, an ascension, that I never knew would take place and ascension that I never knew will prepare me for where I am going today and the International traveling, that has taken place in my life, even now, I had no idea prior to that, that those events would occur of me, traveling the world. But it was in that ascension, that I learned. The power of going higher in God. And that God has an acceleration for our lives that sometimes we don't even know how he will bring. But it is in that ascension, that we grow, and that we develop, and all the specialties of what God has for our lives, and that we understand that in our growing in our developing in our becoming stronger in our becoming wiser, that we are then lifted higher into what God has for our lives.

As I flew on that airplane. And we ascended into the clouds I was able to see in the sky and to observe the beauty of what it was like for the first time in my life to be in an airplane flying soaring and seeing the world. Never seen for the first time. As we flew over the crystal blue waters in Jamaica. I was so astonished by what I saw through the window. It was so beautiful. I was so excited to be in a country that I had never been in before. I thought about the unknown of what was there, who was there, the food, the culture, the people what was it like I was looking forward to learning and seeing all that was there.

Going to Jamaica was my first time that I will know and understand the international call upon my life to reach the world. It was at a young age. That is, send it into the purpose that God had for me. Although God had called me at the age of 13 to preach the gospel. I was now prepared to see other countries. The fact that I have found favor with going with this powerful couple to Jamaica. I was just thankful that they had selected me that they could have chosen anyone to come with them, but they had chosen me to go that lets me know that I was chosen by God. At that time, to fulfill a great purpose in the earth, and that even as a teenager, that I was called.

I was chosen. I was anointed. I was appointed to do all that God had called me to do in that God will say, come forth ascend go higher, go deeper and expand into all that I have for your life. I would like to take you on a flight plan journey today. As you learn about the ascension of what God has for your life. When you understand that you are called. You are chosen. You are anointed, you are appointed to go higher in God and this season, that God is accelerating your purpose. God is accelerating your life. God is taking you to a deeper realm of the Spirit. God is taking you higher and the things of him for such a time as this because there is an acceleration that he wants to do inside of you, to bring you higher so that you may understand that in going higher that you soar as an eagle that he has called you to be as you soar as that wise man or woman of God, that He has called you to be that you soar.

And all that God has called you unto in this season. The one thing that I love about having a flight plan is that it secures you. It protects you. And it covers you and God wants to give each of us today, a flight plan to protect us to cover us to secure us and help us to become all that we need to be in him. When you think about your lineage of where you've come from in life and you think of the journey where God is taking you, you can never imagine the possibilities because they're endless of where God will take you. You must ask yourself, Am I prepared. Am I ready? Am I trained in my mentored? Am I developed enough to do all you've asked me God is my plan, one that I can follow from your leading?

Have you given me the guidance and the tools that have prepared me for what I'm getting ready to do? I want you to know today that God is preparing you. He's preparing you for that Ascension that as you begin to take off on the plane of your life to your journey and destination of where God is having you to go in that you've already secured, your luggage that you've already. Fasten your seat belt. You've already prepared the way for where God is taking you because you know in your heart that as you begin to ascend. As you begin to soar. As you begin to move in the realm of the spirit that there is a place of deeper. There's a place of higher. There's a place of more than expected that you've prayed for so long. So, God wants to give that to you today, a place of more, a place of ascension, a place of going higher, a place of going deeper for such a time as this for His glory. Maybe you have always dreamed of ascending in going higher. Maybe you were looking to find out more about Ascension in your life. This is the time that God has preordained that God has destined for you to go higher, for you to go deeper, for you to develop that relationship that you've prayed on for you to develop that passion, that God has given unto you that in your flight plan that you were secured, that you are prepared, and you are ready to ascend into all that God has for you and more.

The flight plan is to be taken seriously. God is giving you a checklist of things to do. As you prepare, so that you become ready, that you just don't jump into ministry, jump into your calling jump into what is asked of you, but that you take proper precaution, that you prepare for your ascension. That you pack lightly. For the things that he's causes and to do that you prepare with prayer that you prepare with fasting. As you prepare with a good church that will help build you to help you grow into things of him. As you prepare to be studying and reading the Word and building yourself up daily. As you prepare with learning and development to grow even more and God. In that, as you learn, grow and develop, you gain a better understanding of yourself daily. Because now you would have acquired and understood what it means to ascend. What it means to go higher.

What it means to go deeper in the realm of the Spirit. What it means to go higher in your prayer life. Some of you have never taken the time to pray for more than one hour. This is your time to accelerate and propel and go deeper in your prayer life deeper in your relationship with God, deeper in the things that God has for you, deeper. So that in deeper. You, in fact, will grow and develop into all that God has for you. This is your time of ascension. This is your time have a celebration, the checklist is important to have, because in that. It prepares you for the journey that lies ahead. It prepares you for the leaps that you are about to take it prepares you for the journey that God has given for such a time as this. There will be many coaches, mentors, and trainers during this time to coach you, and prepare you for your journey in the Holy Spirit will be there. Also, to bring back to remembrance, everything that you've learned and been trained in to do. So, in this flight plan. It is the first part of the journey ahead, and that it prepares. Is it sets the tone of where you're going in your acceleration, it sets the tone of where you'll be? It lets you know that you're going to go higher. You're going to ascend. You're going to learn how to ascend. You're going to learn everything you need to know and the ascension to go deeper.

Every flight that I have ever flown on consisted of first having a plan in place to go on a trip and having a destination in mind that I would be traveling to. Without a plan and a destination as the two go hand in hand there was not a destination to descend to. In Jeremiah 29:11 it states, "For I know the plans that I have for you declares the

Lord, plans to prosper you and not to harm you, plans to give you hope and a future." Planning in life can sometimes become one to some that is a tedious process.

Having a God-ordained plan is place is most demonstrational in our success in life and in our growth and development in Christ. A plan stands as a preparation tool that begins the process of change and implementation in our life. The same goes to same with a flight plan it requires substantial preparation and a complete dedication to knowing that the plan that is being derived is going to affect and to change lives.

What plans have you implemented in you versus the plans that God has implemented in your life. The plans that we have may not always be the plans that God has for us. What are some plans that you have allowed yourself to plan and never follow up on or adhere to? How can you then create a plan that is in line accordingly? In order to ascend you must first establish a flight plan of action that is in accordance with the word of God and then allow the ascension and plan that God has for your life to help you to flow into the master plan that he has for your life. There is no greater plan and purpose than the purpose and the plan that heavenly father has granted for our lives. It is in his life that we find out the plan and purpose for our lives and create a place of peace that is demonstrated in our trust towards God with his life. In order to flow in a proper plan, we must trust the process of the plan first and then we must trust the pilot and the flight crew that are there to get us to our destination and to serve us accordingly. Who have you trusted with your life today? Who have you allowed to take you to the next destination in your life and cause you to soar to new heights and new debts? There is such a great plan that God has for your life and he wants to see you soar in this season and he wants to see you go higher in your life than you ever have before.

The timing of God is not like our timing his timing goes so much deeper than we can ever imagine. God's timing for your life and his plan for your life is to help you plan towards your new place in through proper preparation, prayer and fasting and seeking his word accordingly. There is a great power that resonates within us when we surrender our hearts to God and give over our plans so that his plans can be executed in our lives. There is so much that Heavenly father wants to breathe into our lives in this season as we are accelerating and moving in the things of him. There are many dimensions that are correlated into the acceleration process in which we will discuss in its entirety in this book.

The first of which includes the first dimension of having a flight plan. This may be like some in having an action plan, but the flight plan is powerful in that it is first executed and birthed out in prayer and then properly alluded to become the final trademark stamp for our destiny. We can become liberated and step into the freedom and promises of the Lord when we set a stage and time of our lives over to God in surrender and allow him to have full coarse and reign over our future and our destiny. It helps to exhibit the true order and mastery of Christ in that his power becomes so real in our lives when we recognize and spend and share the time with him in prayer and praise for the plan that is being birthed out. We must allow Holy Spirit to speak to us and empower us to become all that we need to be in Christ.

When we do see we are then in full surrender to God and he can then pour out his purposes in us more clearly and we can also see the power of God demonstrated in our lives in a way that we may never have experienced before. It's time to ascend higher and to rise into the deeper place in God and to understand the power that is unlocked in acceleration. When we come to terms of the dynamic plan of God for our lives and we begin to see the fruit of our labor as it is birthed out and magnified for the glory of God, we can then experience the true favor and promises of the Lord in our lives.

We must have a desire to want to go deeper and to long for more of what God wants in our lives versus what we want in our lives. We must have a desire that stretches us in its entirety to become the men and women of God that want to be children of God that developed in such a way that the vision and power of God is emulated to be that of vision, passion and persistence to the things of God in this hour. That is something that may people have fallen prey to lacking within the body of Christ is vision and persistence.

We are where we are in our walk with God and in our faith because we have not allowed ourselves to become stretched and to go higher in God. Ascending into the promises and purposes of God involves all encompasses all these facets. We must have desire so deep inside of us that stretches for more of God and we must have a desire that says that the plans of God will outweigh our plans in this hour because the purpose of God is just that dynamic and the future that is coming because of it that involves souls and people that we are to reach and to connect to is engrafted fully in our quest for the things of God that are more impactful to our lives. There must be a true passion and desire in our lives to see the fulness and promises of God executed and displayed in our lives and it is created and accomplished when we are in absolute surrender to God and we have a desire to succeed and to grow more and to also see the plans that are arising and going forth in our lives as we truly connect and plan for all that God has for us and more in this season.

In this season of our lives, we must have a declaration passion for more of God that screams louder than anything in this world and that

Accelerate

Dr. Monique Rodgers

impacts all around us that we may encounter. There is such a profound hope in knowing that in our planning and in our preparation that we are going to experience such a magnitude of growth in the process. When we truly take the time to go deeper and to really soar into the things of God, we open a window of Heaven that creates an undying hope for not just ourselves but to those around us. There is such a great power in planning and God has gifted many of us with the gift of administration that helps to make the planning process seamless.

When God spoke to me and said the words Accelerate in 2017 it propelled me to open a group on Facebook called, I commit to live sold out to God in 2017 and since then the group is still growing and we now have over 1,000 members in it because wanted to do something beyond my plans and beyond my normalizations of life for his glory. God has accelerated me in ministry, in writing, in leadership, in singing, in the prophetic, in the apostolic, and in his purpose for my life. In order to get to where we need to be in God, we must have a flight plan in place and know that what are going to carry on the plane of life with us and who will be a part of our flight crew and who we will leave behind that is causing extra baggage in our lives. We must move out distractions and confusion and replace it with things that bring life to us and that help us to reach our plans in God in an excellent manner. There are so many things in my life that God has helped me to accomplish and leap forward into in my life and it has only been because caused me to plummet into them through his great love for my life and through realizing that the plan and promises of God are real and that there is nothing that can separate my life from the love of God and his plans for life as it is for your life as well there is nothing that can stand in the way of the promises of God for your life and you have to know during this time that God has created and designed a flight plan that is specifically tailored for your life during this time that no one can take away or cause you to deter from because there is such a great call and purpose on your life to walk in the plan that he has for your life and it far exceeds any other plans that we may make for ourselves here on earth.

The plans that are established are the plans that have been fully executed and designed with God in mind. We have to push pass our wants and desires and how we plan to initiate something and trust the process of God and see him magnified in our lives when we give our plans over to God and we have to trust him and really understand that he is the Lord over our lives and as great as it is to create millions of plans the one that really stands out is the plan that God has specifically aligned for our lives so that we may walk in into it with great boldness and truth and knowing that he is able to see us through every plan in our lives and to help us to rise above every challenge and every act of warfare that will try to come in and deter the plans of God on our lives. We have to know and realize that his plans are far greater that we can ever imagine and we have to learn that in trusting the process and the plan of God that we are in absolute surrender to his will and to his purpose for our lives and it does not cause use to become weak in a negative manner instead it helps us to arise and conquer in God when we have completely given our plans over to the Lord and acknowledged him as the ultimate planner of our lives.

Chapter Two

Pack Lightly & Go Deeper in God

Every trip that I have ever traveled on I have found myself to always overpack. I then try repacking only to find that I still have packed more than what was intended for the trip. At the same notion however, I have also discovered and found close friends and family members that were masters of packing so to speak. I have seen some even label the outfits that were being worn and put garments in Ziplock bags neatly and poised and every item is folded extra carefully within each bag. I have flown all over the world and have rolled clothes, folded clothes and even at the last minute have thrown items into a bag and traveled. What I have discovered upon this packaging process is the lighter the luggage the easier it was for me to carry the bags that were unchecked around the airport, train station or bus station.

Packing lightly is especially essential for flying because the extra baggage that is carried causes more time to attend to and less time to spend doing things that matter the most in the airport. So is the same for the spiritual. The more we carry around baggage from 2020 and years past of what we have been through and suffered from the more we become even more weighed down and burdened with our time and with our lives. Baggage weighs us down whether it is in the natural or the spiritual. In Hebrews 12:1 it says, "Wherefore seeing we also are compassed about with so great a cloud of witnesses, let us lay aside every weight, and the sin which doth so easily beset us, and let us run with patience the race that is set before us."

Whenever we are weighed down with baggage of gossip, past pains and issues, other people's problems and life in general we cannot ascend higher in our lives because of the weight of the baggage that is holding us back from reaching our destiny. It is hard to move forward when we have heavy bags that are being held like bricks and chains to our legs. It is hard to propel into anything that God has given us when we are locked in bondage to our past, to mental bondage, to life and to others who do not want to go higher in life. These kinds of situations hold us hostage to forfeiting our rights to our final destinations that we are embarking upon. The weightier we become from life barriers the

25

more tied down to it we will then be causing us to move backwards as opposed in forward motion. God is calling us higher in this season is calling you by name and telling you to ascend higher and to go forth in all that he has for your life and more.

God is asking us to not get distracted with baggage in our lives but to continue to move forward and to go ascend deeper into the things that God has intended for our lives. The moment we release the extra baggage that is when things will start to release in our lives that has been held up for years. God wants to deliver us and bring us to our land of blessings and promise and free us from the pit of disparity and baggage. God is trying to stretch us forth and help us to go higher into the promises that he has for our lives, but we are stuck on last year's disappointments and last year's blessings. It's time to ascend higher onto higher thinking patterns and higher realms in the spirit. God has so much that he wants to reveal to us and to show us, but we are too caught up in our issues or someone else's issue to find out what he must reveal to us.

God wants to deliver us from the place us stuck to the place of movement. If there is too much baggage holding us down from reaching our purpose, we can't ascend or go higher because of the problems that have us completely held up. Some of us are being held up to mental baggage of our past that we really need to release and give to God. Others are being loaded down with life by putting too much in our bags that we know that we must out of our lives and our bags. Some of us are loading our bags with things that are harmful to our lives and detrimental to us going ever going forward in God. God is stopping and doing a radar check on our lives today to ensure that we are ready for the ascension. He has literally stopped us like we are at TSA to scan and check the baggage that we have been carrying and thinking it was okay carry.

God does not want you to continue being loaded down with things that are locked into your purpose. Extra baggage of time wasters, extra baggage of depression, extra baggage of fear, extra baggage of people that do not want to go higher. The radar of the Holy Spirit checker is alarming in your life to alert you to let go of the baggage and to get the true freedom in your life in God that will bring you to ascension. In order to accelerate its going to take releasing some things are a dead weight to our lives. It's going to take walking away from people, places, and things that are detrimental to your purpose. The more time that we spend holding on to dead things the more time we are taking away from reaching the true propensity of what God has given unto to us.

Some of us are one step closer to reaching our purpose and others are one connecting flight away from reaching their destiny to connect to their purpose. What took some people years to experience or learn God wants to give to us in months or weeks. God has accelerated my life in so many ways. He told me that I would do more in my lifetime that some have thought of doing for years. I am so honored at where God has shifted and taken my life and the new journey that he has me embarking on. The major connections that he has given me and all the destiny helpers that he has surrounded me with to help to support my vision and goals for my life. God told me that he was accelerating things in my life and in the lives of others in 2021 that this would be the year of congratulatory moments of success

I see that happening now in my life. The ascension that God is leading me on is so powerful and I am humbled and honored at what God is doing in my life. This year alone I have finished a mentorship program called Exodus 3, I was nominated for Who's Who in 2021, I was inducted into The International Society of Female Professionals, I was coauthor in a book that made number one release and best seller on Amazon. I also am about to finish a dual Doctorate degree in Theology and Ministry this month.

When God told me that my life would be an example of acceleration, he has truly shown that in so many ways through the favor that he has already released on my life. What would take some people years to complete God has allowed me to complete in weeks or months and I am so grateful for the accelerated path that he has extended to my life.

God spoke to me in this year that I need take my love even farther and grow deeper in my relationship with Him. I had to understand that there was a point that I needed to go deeper, deeper and my relationship with God deeper in my thought patterns deeper in my knowing that there was more to what God had for my life. In order to understand what going deeper meant, at first have had to investigate the definition of deep and understand the power of what it means to go deeper. And in finding that I understood then that deep meant to extend far down from the top or surface, very intense, or extreme.

And then to follow on to that I understood even further that going deep meant extending far from some surface or area, such as an extending far downward, a deep well, a deep chasm, extending well inward from an outer surface, a deep gash or deep, says the animal. When I investigate the word deep and makes me further in my thoughts of knowing that there's something far greater, that is inside of me, When I look at the word deeper, it also helps me to understand that in the intensity of the deep, that is there, there's always the after effect of what comes from going beyond.

What I mean by that is that in the beyond is the furnace of

going more inside of the surface area of our life, we must search for what is deeper inside of us, we must look for those broken places, we must look for the broken parts that needs to be fixed, and we must work on fixing them. Because If we don't, we lose out on healing, we lose out on relationships, we lose out on love. Now, that's not to say that God is not going to continue to love us, that is not something that will happen because God will continue to love you.

But The more that you begin to love yourself, and you're able to love others, you can step out of the box of where you are, and your deep pattern thoughts of what love should be or what love should look like or how love exists, it's so long for you that you're able to really evolve and feel the effectiveness of what is involved in love. And What I mean by that is you must go deeper and find out what that is, you must search for what the purpose is for that deepness, you must look beyond the level of what that love was before and see what that love has now become. When I did this, I was able to understand that going deeper and my relationship with God was important.

It was not something that I regretted or didn't feel that I need it. But it's something that I wanted for my life. Because I wanted to experience God's love just that great. I wanted to experience His love beyond the surface area, I wanted to experience His love in a way that I had never experienced before. And the only way to do that was to get raw with myself to look at myself in the mirror and say how much do I want to be loved? How much do I want to be accepted? How much do I want to be changed? How much do I want to go deep deeply in my walk with the Lord? And that is not always easy for me. It's not always easy for anyone.

And if it is easy for you, then that's a wonderful thing. But when you must really stretch yourself and go beyond what you're used to, and start really pushing into what felt good before, and then move past that and then go into what feels even better. Now, That's a stretch. Because anytime that you stretch yourself, you are pulling the last city of what you experienced beforehand, into a deeper gratitude of what you're experiencing now. Because it pulls you in allows you to be stretched, it's kind of like that of a rubber band being stretched, because you must end the rubber band stretching the material as to the pic on itself to be even stretched forward. So that is what God has done for me in this season. He has allowed me to be stretched like that rubber band, he's allowed me to not pop to not snap to not lose it, and the process of all that I've gone through. Because it can be so impactful that you know, you can lose your mind in the process of the things that you're going through.

But God holds their mind together, He holds you together because he loves you just that much, He wants to see you developed, he wants to see you process and grow and to all that He has for you like you cannot get to where you supposed to be by holding on to what was what could have been. The way that you go deeper is by going beyond the surface level of where you are, and propelling yourself into what you need to be in.

And when we go to a deeper level, and God, we're able to experience that because then our purpose becomes not just on the outer level, but it becomes even more deeper to what God has called us into.

The reason why you are reading this book today may not be the reason why someone else is reading it. The reason that someone else picked this book up men may have been the cover may have been the title may have been because they had been through pain in their life, maybe they have experienced a pattern and a lot that they don't understand why they went through. But for whatever reason you are reading this, I'm thankful for it.

But God wants to thank you even more, because he wants to let you know that is not by accident that you have picked up this book today is not by accident that you have gone beyond the pages, and to this chapter that you're in Now the last chapter of this book, that he has begun to even revelation to you why you are reading this book. God has a purpose for you and his purpose.

He wants you to know and understand that there is a deeper call to your life, there is a deeper level of love that you are reaching your life, there is a deeper promise that God will extend to your life. But you must be willing to step out of the area that you're in now and embrace what he is taking you. There was so much stretching that has happened in my life, even down to the level of how I am eating in my life. Now God even shifted me to becoming a vegan.

Now That to me was a complete stretch. Because I had been used to eating chicken. I've been used to eating fried foods I've been used to eating French fries and pizza. So that was a complete stretch from my life. But in the shifting of the eating pattern that God has me on to being a vegan, I've developed even more better than my health, my cholesterol has decrease. And I feel a lot better physically.

And I look a lot younger physically, because of the God, God, being obedient to God, and allowing him to tell me what to eat during that time and how to save my health and how to save my life. So, all the things that I've gone through in my life have not been by accident, even in the area of the birth, functioning of my life, you know, even the birth order of being the middle child, God knew that there are some things that I need to push my sister into, and to push my brother into.

The only way that he can allow me to do that he was strategic in the planning of the process of where he positioned me and where he placed me and where he put me so that I would know that there was more to what he had in store.

And God is really pushing me even further now to let me know that if I'm going to be all in for him, or I'm going to be all out for him, because I need to know and develop inside of myself that I am going to be all out for the Lord, I'm going to go live my life sold out for him so deeply that it doesn't matter anymore what people say or what people think, or what they're expressing towards me, because I have to know that the love that God has inside of me is far greater than what anyone can say, or do or try to harm me or do to me in the process.

And I had to break free from the opinions of others. You know, in doing that it's a process because we feel that we must appease people, we must please them. So, God is showing me during this time that I don't have to please people anymore, that I don't have to live my life up to the standards of man. But the only standards that I had to live up to is the standards of God, His love for my life has loved me to the point of knowing that that I had to break free into His presence into his love, and to his grace, and to his companionship from my life and not my own. So there has come an expectancy with that There's come the expectancy of knowing God's love for my life, there's come to expect to see a knowing that I am Furthermore, and looking forward to being loved daily, I'm looking forward to being love even more because of God because of his love for my life. And that is how we must live our lives in the expectancy of His love, the expectancy of His grace, the expectancy of what He has promised to us.

And I know that in the everlasting grace of God's love for me that there's so much more because when I look at the word everlasting, that to me, represents so much more than my finite mind could ever think. Because when you think of the word everlasting, that is powerful, that means lasting forever, for a long time. So, the knowing that God's love for me is everlasting. That is powerful, because that means that it's going to go from now to eternity, that there's no ending

Dr. Monique

to it, that there's nothing that I can do to end that because His love is for me.

So that is the everlasting promise that God has for our lives is the everlasting grace of his love for us. And when we have that great love in our lives, we're able to experience the power of what he has brought us to where he has birthed us into. And now it's not always an easy process of knowing that, but it has taken me in my lifetime now to experience that. And I'm grateful for this, because God's love is just so beautiful to me.

And I'm able to experience His love and the magnitude now that I've never been able to experience before, because I've opened myself up to be loved and to receive love and to go further in the love of God. And because of this love, I've been known that there is a Promise of Hope beyond this, that I'm looking to be in the everlasting love that He has for my life. And I'm hoping that that is the same that you're wanting for your life is to experience the everlasting love that He has for you.

Be everlasting love that He has given to you the everlasting

38

love that he wants to pour you the everlasting love that he wants to shower on you today Be everlasting love that he wants to extend to you today. You must know in yourself that there is so much more to where your life has been, and where you're going and where you want to go when you want God to take you. This is my story is not the same as yours is not always going to be the same as anyone else's. Because your story is not always designed to be with someone else's story is. And so, in that you must know that there's purpose.

There's love, and there's grace, and there's everlasting love for your life. You must look to receive that you must look to understand that you must look to believe that and know that and gravitate to that promise of what God has for your life and really knowing that in his promise, there's so much grace towards you. And there's so much that he wants to do in the process of it all.

So, take thought on this today and really sit back and ponder on the love of God for your life. The love of God for your life, Not anyone else's life, but for your life. And really come to understand and know that there's power and love, that there's grace in love, that there's truth and love, that there's healing and love and that God's love for you is just that valuable, that when you learn to really grow in love and find completion and love. You will then receive the full love of God in your life. Remember to pack lightly and draw deeper to God in this season than you could ever have imagined.

Chapter Three

Pick Your Travel Partners Well

When Jesus picked his twelve disciples, he was very selective in the process. The key thing to remember is that each disciple carried a purpose on their lives. From the friends in your circle that mean you well to the ones that you know are a straight up Judas they each serve a purpose within our lives and the significance of each relationship is what is most important in the selection process as it pertains specifically to your life and the lives of others that you will essentially meet and connect with in life that are a part of your purpose.

I have never had a hard time making friends because I love people and I connect well with others. The problem then for me has been in keeping friends for long periods of time. I have some friends in my circle that have been there for years while others are new to my circle. Some have left, others have walked away by choice and others have moved on to other things and friends.

Picking the right travel partner can be a hard selection process in that you want the person that is rolling with you so to speak to be on that you can have fun with, relate with, be yourself and that you do not mind spending hours with on a plane. The travel partner will not go well if they are one that is a complainer, gossiper, lazy, untrustworthy, procrastinator, or one that does not enjoy traveling. You want people that are traveling with you to want to be there with you. You should have someone like a Peter in your life that is willing to fight for you if anything goes down in your life.

Then you need someone like John in your life that is loyal and that can relate as well as provide revelation on some areas in your life. Then you need a friend like James that will have the faith needed to help you to endure in your flight. The people that we select on your journeys in life should individuals that we are either helping to develop on their journey or someone that is pushing us to propel forward.

When we select individuals that are either time wasters and have no implied interest of traveling it causes us to experience flight delays, aborted travel plans, and never reaching our destination. There is nothing worse that preparing for a trip with someone only to find out that they never intended on going. Things like this delay the process of meeting the accelerated place of where God has for our lives. God has helped me to now become very selective in my friendship circles and my travel circles because even in making a road trip it can sometimes become one that is well remembered for good or well-remembered for what we do not want to occur in the future.

God wants us to connect and network with others, but he also wants us to be wise in our connections and in our relationships. The connectors in our lives are essential to the next place that we are going. Along your destination in life, you will have the opportunity to meet and connect with several people. The important thing to remember in the connection is the importance of why God is allowing the connection and the purpose behind it. Everyone is not meant to be with us forever but the ones that are we should really cherish and celebrate the relationship and cultivate it even the more.

Travel relationships are probably not the easiest at times to select especially if it is a trip that has not been planned and its last minute, we end up asking for the first person that we can find to come on the trip with us to keep up company. Sometimes God won't allow us to have a travel partner because he wants to reveal some things to us along the journey that we need to hear directly from him. It's a time to quiet ourselves before God and to hear what he is speaking and not the sounds from our air pods with music or texts we are sending to others or the noise cancellation headphones that block transmission of sound altogether.

In each still moment that we can capture in our times of travel we are able to hear what God wants us to do and how he wants us to do it. In 2 Chronicles 20:30 it says, "So, the realm of Jehoshaphat was quiet: for his God gave him rest round about." We are often in a battle with our thoughts and with our lives and God just wants us to quiet our spirits for a moment to hear him. Sometimes our next accelerated moment is found right in the tender quiet moments that we spend with God.

Sometimes we delay our acceleration through picking the wrong life partners for marriages. In Proverbs 18:22 it says, "A man that findeth a wife findeth a good thing and obtained favor of the Lord." When the partnership of traveling is aligned with our life partners that are our husband and or our wives it then becomes a travel of ease because the other partner is there to support the other. Couples are fun to travel with because they hold a special connection to one another, and they are used to being together and they hold a special bond of intimacy.

I also admire husbands and wives that travel together and hold hands it just shows such a loyalty of connection through the love that they each share for one another. The husband that connects with the right wife finds favor from God and he also finds peace. The right spouse is going to create a place of ease for our lives that will help us to ascend to the higher places that we have planned to go to.

We can often get slowed down by past relationships, or bad engagements or even drama from our previous marriages for some but it's imperative to have the connected spouse that is in our lives for the long haul and that is truly committed to seeing us reach all that God has for our lives as a couple and as singles.

Ask God to give you clear discernment and insight into the relationships for your lives and ask for love lasting covenant relationships that are substantial for your life. Life is too short to play games or waste time with people who want to play games with their lives. We have a destination that we are trying to obtain and in order to get there we must ascend well prior to getting to the destination.

Every relationship has its ups or downs whether it is friends, family or marriage. We must know who to take with us and when to take them with us. At times in our lives, we may travel with children or grandchildren and we must know if we were supposed to bring them or leave them in proper care. Learning the potential distractors in our lives can help us to alleviate a lot of the chaos in our lives that we often encounter. The correct travel partner will help us along the journey and add value and joy to the travel and less stress.

Chapter Four

Keep the Onboarding Process Secure

How secure are we in our faith and in our walk with God? Is what is keeping us from ascending our fear that has held us hostage or ourselves? As women and men of God we must continually make sure that we are securing our lives daily with God in prayer and protection as well as speaking the word. As prophets. We have been called to sound the alarm to the nations, and to let the world know what God is saying. We are that voice, the voice that needs to be heard the voice that operates through a prophetic sound through a clarion call for people all over the world to hear into understand, of what God is saying. He uses his chosen prophets to deliver that word, and to get it out to those that are in need. Equitation.

The warning encouraged. Rise prophets. It's time to speak and declare what God is saying to the world. It's time for you to be that voice that prophetic voice that delivers the Word of God to his people. It helps them to understand what the signs of the times are and gives

47

us the deep revelation that is imparted through God through His Word. It's not time anymore. For prophets to sit on the sidelines and just watch as the world crumbles away, but it's time for prophets to arise to speak the Word of God to declare to the nations, what God is saying to these people. And to do it without fear to do it without trepidation to do it without self-gain and gratification. Let's deliver a word to God's people that will sustain them.

That will keep them. That will comfort them. That will deliver them, and that will bring them out of the fiery pit profits. You walk in a higher call in that you are servants of the Highest God, and He delights you. The Word of God says he did. He reveals the secrets to his profits. You are those profits. You are the ones that God is speaking to today to declare the word from Almighty God, to the world. You haven't been called to sit with a muzzle on your mouth.

And no one hears you. But you've been called to set the tone to the prophetic word that is uttered through your voice. You have been called for such a time as this to rise and to stand on the promises of Jesus Christ. And no longer sit on the sidelines of fear and doubt and discontent and worry. It's time to awaken arise profit and go forth in the things that wish God has called you to go into to use your prophetic voice to speak life over the dead situations that approach you to speak life over the things that are dead surrounding you to speak life over the dead situations that are becoming to you.

It's time to hear. To see to speak to declare what God is saying. As an oracle of God. You were chosen to do that, to speak the word to be that word. To show that worthy your actions profit. Oh, guys profit. Take on your rightful place. Don't look to the left. Don't look to the right. But look ahead at what God is doing it what God is saying.

He's calling for people to stand firm on the truth. To not dilute the Word of God. But just to clear the truth. That is the word of God. As prophets we are to stand with that word in our mouths daily. And not water it down, but to keep it as a burning fire. I was sounding torch that never goes out to deliver to the people. God's people what he's saying. It's time to walk in to declare to the world. Wake up. Wake up from your sleepy slumber, wake up from your clouded vision, wake up from your clogged ears. Wake up from your stiff-necked routine. Wake up from your ill hurt procedures, wake up from things that are casual and not fixated on the things of God. Follow the voice of God. During this time, be that prophetic voice that God hears, and that the world hears. Let your voice. Carry flame, like a torch that never goes out, so that the world hears the fire through your voice. In catches it. And they too can feel the passion of Christ. For the words that you speak.

Chapter Five

In Flight Menu/ What are you feeding your spirit man?

One of the greatest joys that I loved about international traveling was the food that we eat on the ride. The longer the flight length the better food that is given. This was prior to the pandemic and the flight restrictions that we now have on board. There's so much that you must understand when you want to really grow in your relationship with God. It takes time. It takes patience. It takes love. And it takes you really wanting to grow for what you have gone through in your life is not always easy. And if we expect it to be easy, then we're looking for something that doesn't exist. And in God's love, is surely the existence that you need. Because His love, extends grace, extends peace. Extends patience extends the love that we need for our lives.

When I look at where I've come from, and where God has taken me, I understand that in the abuse, in the hurt, in the eating

51

disorders, In the misunderstanding, in the abandonment, In the search for answers to love, that I was then able to gravitate to the real love of Christ my life. It wasn't in love of man or the love in others, or the love in what I could thought I could extinguish myself. But it was solely in the love of God, that I found his love for me. And maybe you're at that place right now. Yet you're standing in, and you don't recognize that God loves you. And that there are no strings attached, that there is simply love only for you. You must know that you are loved. You must know that there is so much power in the love that God has for you. You must know that his love is so deeply for you that it can never be changed.

It can never be disrupted, it can never be erased, because it's that powerful. The same God that fought for my love is the same God that will fight for you. The same God that helped me to recover from shame is the same God that will help you to recover from what you're going through. The same God that helped and healed me to a mask every area of my life that I was feeling that I had to cover and keep hidden in my life is the same God that will build those pieces inside of you and bring you to the complete deliverance that you need for your life. Stop hiding and start a Brit embracing what God has for you. Is so beautiful when you allow God to heal your wounds instead of yourself. When you allow God to heal those broken areas and not run away from them. You ever just wanted to feel love? Have you ever just wanted to experience love? Have you ever just wanted to fall in love again? It can happen. Because in God's love is endless. In God's love. He wants to give you those intimate moments with him.

And God's love. He wants to shower you and position you for the promise for your life And God's love. He wants to take you deeper with a purpose in mind, and God's love. He wants to show that you can go all in for His glory. In God's law is where the promise for your life extends. You must learn to break free into the promise to love. You must learn that there is so much power and expectancy of the love of God for your life, that you are now reckoning to flow even more in his love. Because in the everlasting promise that he has for your life, you can then grow and gravitate to that love by being all that he wants you to be and more.

It's time for me to stretch. It's time for me to grow in my love for the Lord. It's time for me to become intimate more with him. And to understand the intimate moments of promise that are available for my life. It's time for me to really dive in and stop waiting on something and go after what he has my life. It's time for me really to go into the intimate secret closet places the promises that the Lord has for my life, and really searched to develop and growth as a woman of God that He has called me to be during the season. There's no more time to waste. There's no more time to wait. There's no more time to linger and under Try to understand what the problem is. But to really focus on what God has called me to do. I can't focus on what does not exist in my life. I cannot focus on what I wish I could have had and what I could have done better.

But The thing that I must hold on to is the promise of God's love in my life, the promise of hit the intimacy that I will now embrace in my life, the promise of the joy and celebration of knowing that all that happened before does not have to be a part of my life any longer.

Dr. Monique Rodgers

And it's now a time for me to go deeper in the promises of what God has in my mind and in my emotions and in my purpose. I know that my life exudes Jesus. There's no turning back. There is no looking back. There's no stepping back. I am all in because he is all in for me and I'm going to give all my love for him. It is a cherish time of diving in pressing forward that I understand the promises now that God has in my life. I'm going to be even more of my food careful of the food selection choices that I make for my spirit because I want to satisfy and feed my spirit man with things that are uplifting and that bring me life.

Chapter Six

Fasten Your Seatbelts

The most fascinating part of going on a plane ride is the take off. The takeoff determines how smooth the landing will be in the end. Like the plane taking off like the plane in motion has also been the takeoff of a roller coaster is similar in that it goes so fast and it creates an exhilarating experience and ends with a smooth landing. The captain always has their passengers to fasten their seatbelts and sends the flight attendants to check to see if everyone has their seatbelts on. The flight crew then assembles to ensure that each passenger is securely fastened and that they are safe. That is how God attends to us as his sons and daughters. He ensures that we are safe and that we are secure.

The tightened seatbelt ensures that as the word says in Psalm 91:1-10 it says, "He that dwelleth in the secret place of the most High shall abide under the shadow of the Almighty. I will say of the Lord,

He is my refuge and my fortress: my God; in him will I trust. Surely,
he shall deliver thee from the snare of the fowler, and from the
noisome pestilence. He shall cover thee with his feathers, and under
his wings shalt thou trust: his truth shall be thy shield and buckler.
Thou shalt not be afraid for the terror by night; nor for the arrow that
flieth by day; Nor for the pestilence that walketh in darkness; nor for
the destruction that wasteth at noonday.

A thousand shall fall at thy side, and ten thousand at thy right
hand; but it shall not come nigh thee. Only with thine eyes shalt thou
behold and see the reward of the wicked. Because thou hast made the
Lord, which is my refuge, even the Highest, thy habitation; There shall
no evil befall thee, neither shall any plague come nigh thy dwelling."
In the safety and protection of our father God is hope, trust, and love.
When we are affirmed and loved by God, we are secure in what he has
called us to do from the acknowledgement and the display of his love
for us. When we formulate in our minds the importance of being
secure in our identity with God and in our walk with Christ it helps us

to walk out the true purpose to which we are called to in our lives.

Like that of a baby needing the security and assurance of his or her mother that is the same how we are dependent on our Father God. The needs are evident, and we are not ashamed to show that we need God or that we are longing for the assurance of his word in our lives. When we are at a place of vulnerability and surrender to God, he can unlock the windows of Heaven in our lives and cause of to walk into a place of complete surrender.

On the contrary when we are not in tuned to the alignment and passage of what is doing in our lives, we can very easily miss out on the accelerated moment that is about to happen and to occur in our lives. When we negate to really press in and understand the safety and protection that comes with Jesus and his Angels. There is a host of Angels that surround us to protect us and to make sure that we are safe and that we are secure in God.

God wants to blanket us is in his assurance of knowing that we are safe and that we are protected and that we are ascending into all that he has for us in this season and in more. The deeper that we dive into his presence and continue to seek his face the more we can draw closer in understanding that what God has given unto to our lives is providing action steps to complete as we are the first partakers of the voyage of where God is taking us into.

Chapter Seven

Prepare for Turbulence

The worst feeling that I have ever felt while riding on an airplane has been that of the turbulence that comes with the flight. The windy places that I have flown into that have had the most turbulence were Chicago, Philadelphia and Tulsa. Every time I have flown into these cities in particular the turbulence on the plane has literally heightened. God wants us to prepare for the turbulent moments in our lives that often catch us unaware. It is in the air pockets and clouds of life as we ascend that the turbulent moments happen the most.

Turbulence comes in moments in our lives wherein we least expect it and it cause us to feel like the tumultuous adversity that we are experiencing is one of a personal attack that is sent specifically to distract and deter us from our destinies. Turbulence causes uproars in our lives of waves of challenges that we often have a hard time of facing. God wants to help us through the ever increasing and invasive turbulence in our lives of destruction and help to develop and even greater meaning and understanding of the warfare that you are facing and experiencing now.

In 2 Corinthians 10:4 it says, "The weapons we fight with are not the weapons of the world. On the contrary, they have divine power to demolish strongholds." In Ephesians 6:10 it says, "For our struggle is not against flesh and blood, but against the rulers, against the authorities, against the powers of this dark world and against the spiritual forces of evil in the heavenly realms."

God wants us to be aware and to acknowledge that the attacks are coming and that as they come there shall come a greater victory as you fight in the battle and in the turbulent moments of your life that have shaken you. Maybe you are now in your life now that you feel like the burdens are life are just that overwhelming and that you have nothing left to offer.

God wants you to know today that there is much for you to

offer and that as you go through the mountains and tests of your life that you continue to soar. On the airplane even though there is turbulence you must continue soaring and reaching all that God has for you and more. turbulence. One thing I know and understand about turbulence is that when you are flying in an airplane, and you were riding in the skies, that the pain that you experience in your belly.

At that moment, it lasts for a moment, and then it ends. So that is how the tests and trials come and are alive. They come, they invade, they exist. I tried to keep us in that same moment, wondering when it is going to end. When is the pain going to go away? When is this turbulence going to end? When is all that is happening in my life going to stop? But I must ask myself at that moment, is what I'm experiencing is what I am going through at this moment, so overwhelming that I can't praise God in the process.

What has invaded your life so much at this moment that you are not able to praise God because of it. What are the distractors that are causing you to stand and not face what God is giving you to do? Why are you still in the place of stuck when God is trying to bring you to a place of flourish when the tumultuous times come, you must know and realize that God is aligning your lives for the shifting.

Know and recognize that you're experiencing that God is with you, he's able to bring you through, he's able to bring you out, he's able to bring you to a place of promise, he's able to bring you into a place of peace, to bring you out of that experience that you were in and bring you to a place of peace and clarity and its God. So, we know that when we are in those times that we are in turbulent moments, we are in those times where it is turbulent and everything is shaking around us, where the very ground under US is shaking.

God wants us to know that in those shaking moments, he wants to move the mountains in your life, and those shaky moments that he wants to do a great work in your life, that in those shaking moments, that there is a breakthrough that is taking place and the shaking times that you are experiencing, you have to know and realize that breakthrough is coming, that God has come to free you out of some things that God has come to birth you out of some places that God has come to bring you into a releasing of that moment, that as you begin to step in as you begin to walk in the place that God is taking you that there is such a breakthrough that is going to come, that the tumultuous time that you are experiencing that God wants to bring you out of that moment, and bring you to a place of peace, a place of safety, a place of any his wheel, a place of the buy moment. This is that time, that as you are flying. As you are soaring.

As you are gliding through life, that you begin to experience all that God has for you and more that you begin to experience the peace and safety that God has for your life that you begin to understand and realize the peace of God that passes all understanding, will guide your heart and mind. There is an establishment of peace that is happening in your life even now that it's time to celebrate what God is doing. It's not time to feel sad and sorry about your situation and feel sad and sorry about the moments that shake us, but it's a time to celebrate what God is doing in your life. For this is the time.

Dr. Monique Rodgers

This is the moment. This is the hour. This is a season that you will embrace that God is taking you into a new place in your life that yes, it was shaking. Yes, you heard it. Yes, you went through. Yes, you had shaking moments, but God wants you to know today that there's a peace that's coming. There's a peace. There's a river of peace. There's a river of peace that is coming, that God wants to give you that he wants to place within your life, to let you know today to get you to stand upon the promise and continue to tell you to stand in your faith.

Chapter Eight

The Acceleration Process

The steps to accelerating into your kingdom assignment is as follows:

- Prepare daily with prayer
- Live a fasted life
- Hear God's voice and move with action
- Know your purpose
- Don't get lost in your purpose
- Keep accountability
- Move with the movers and shakers in your life
- Keep a circle that pushes you for even greater

The steps to the acceleration process are ones that God has given to me that have helped to advance my life. These same steps can also help you in your life with God as well as you begin to advance in all that he has for your life. The steps to accelerating into your kingdom assignment is as follows. First, you're going to prepare daily with prayer. How beautiful it is to spend time with God praying and seeking his face daily and coming before His throne with praise and prayer and adoration to his name.

Prayer is everything before God. dictionary.com defines prayer to be a psalm requests for help or expression of things, addressed to God, or an object of worship. Prayer is our communication with God. It is our connection that we have to the Father that we're able to express and prayer, our needs and the things that we need to get done. We pray and seek the face of the Father. It helps us to protect and cover our days.

It helps to protect and cover our family. It helps to prepare and protect those around us. So, as we consistently pray as we continually seek the face of the Father, as we continually go before the throne, that we will always be in a posture of prayer that we will always be in a posture of seeking that will always be in a posture of seeking God first and all that we do. In the book of Matthew 6:33, it says, "Seek ye first the kingdom of God in all His righteousness, and all these things shall be added unto you."

Although we do not seek to gather and to have things are seeking is that we may come to the Father with uplifted hands, and we may come to the Father was seeking hearts that we may come to the Father, acknowledging His will for our lives. So, in order to accelerate in the kingdom, we must have access to the Father, which is to have a relationship with him, which is to be saved and live for the Father, and to be in connection with His Divine Will and establishment for your life. When you have that relationship with God.

When you live a life that is postured to prayer posture to communication posture to live in for God, you are then able to experience all that God has for your life and more. I don't know about you, but I have come to understand the power behind prayer, as an intercessor, my life is with prayer ideally spend time with God because I love him just that much, and I want my life to be an example of who he is in my life, as I constantly pray and spend time to God. It is not always the times of shouting before the Lord, but it's times of just being in that secret place, going into my prayer room, laying on the floor before God, seeking Him continuously. Because I know that in my seeking Him. That I will find the answers of that which I'm looking upon every seeking moment that we have of God, every chance and opportunity that we must seek the face of the father should be one that is sacred to be one that is referenced to be one that is suitable for God because it is our opportunity to seek Him and be before his face. So, as you prepare daily live prayer and your first process of your celebrating moment. I pray that God accelerates your prayer life that he takes your prayer life to the next level that you begin to have an even greater passion for the things of God.

As you begin to have an even greater passion for prayer, and even greater a celebrated life in your prayer life that you spend more time with God, that your answers to your prayer come swiftly that the things that you need in your life or answer, the things that you've been praying about for years are answered swiftly because of the timing of God right now in this season. The next part of the acceleration process is to live a fasted life. I don't know about you, but I remember the first time that I fasted. I was in a room with church mothers, and we were in a shut in at the time. And we were not able to eat anything for three days straight. The moment they told me that there will not be any food, I immediately felt hunger in my belly, because I'm so used to food and I'm so used to eating. So being able to not eat at that time did something to me. And so, I thought, well, this is going to really be a sacrifice for me because this is something I've never done before, but I'm would be opposed to doing I just have never done and I'm a young child, and so why would I do this, but in that moment of being there with those church mothers.

It taught me the power of self-control and being able to condition your body and put it under subjection and being able to put your body in place of subjection to wanting so much more than and dying to my flesh. So, live in a fasted life has taught me that I am that I am able to put aside my flesh, for the things of God, that the things that I want are not as important as the things that God wants that he has a greater purpose and charge in my life that when I fast and pray, I am helping myself to lay aside things that hold me hostage.

Dr. Monique Rodgers

I'm helping myself to become even greater for God, because I'm laying aside those wants and desires that displease him. so, I'm helping to get my life in order. I'm helping my life to become even better, and God by laying aside my wants and needs, so that he can be satisfied and pleased in every way. Another part of the acceleration process is hearing God's voice and moving with action. I don't know about you, but when the big plane begins to take off. There's such a movement that is happening during that time. The wheels are spinning. The plane is moving, you are moving the whole aircraft is moving during that time, and it is an opportunity for action to occur. So, as you begin to hear God's voice. There's a movement, there is an action that is taking place in your life that God is bringing forth through you. In this time and moment of your life, understand that as you begin to hear God's voice more, that there is an action that comes to your hearing his voice that you're not just hearing. Only, but you're doing so God wants you to not only be hearers of the word but to be doers of the word.

So, when we hear what God is saying, what we hear what God

is doing, when we hear what God is asking of us that there's a motion that comes to it. Some of us have been stuck so long that we have not been able to hear God, we've been so stuck in our situation, stuck in a pattern of life, stuck in our slothfulness stuck in places that have taken us under, but God wants to take us over into a place of mobility, a place of movement, a place of motion, a place of going forward, a place of moving forward, a place of moving an action and all that God has your life. This is the action moments that you begin to step in.

This is the action time that you begin to go and this is the action that would you shampoo forward in the season, that this is the acceleration time, that will begin to move with action as you hear God's voice as you hear him with clarity, as you hear him with wisdom that you will begin to walk in it that you'll begin to talk and that you'll begin to live in it, and all that God have called for you to do. The next part of the acceleration process is to know your purpose. I can't tell you how many times I've seen so many people chasing the purpose of others, and not knowing the purpose of that which they have for their lives, in which God has intended. The moment that you find out what your purpose is, and you find out what God has called you to do. You will no longer be chasing the purpose of someone else, but you are rather be chasing the purpose that God is alive for your life.

There's a purpose, that is attached to your life, even now, that God wants you to flow in that God wants you to live in that God wants you to grow in that God wants you to develop in your purpose is now your purpose is for this moment that as you are living out your purpose that you will follow what God has called and intended for you to do. That's your purpose and God will be established that your purpose in God will be lived out on this earth. That's your purpose and God shall come to pass, and some.

In the book of Psalm, 57:2, the word of God says, "I cry out to God most high to God who fulfills his purpose for me." This key in understanding God's purpose for your life is to understand His purpose of what he's called you unto. What is God saying for you to do at this moment. What is he specifically aligned for your life? In Romans 8:28, it says, "And we know that for those who love God, all things work

together for good for those who are called according to His purpose."
In the book of Psalm 138:8 it says, "The Lord will fulfill His purpose
for me, your steadfast love Oh God, endures forever. Do not forsake
the work of your hands." And then the part of having purpose is having
vision and understanding what God has established for your life. There
is an appointed time that God has for you. You are purposed, you are
called, you are chosen your call to walk in the purposes of which God
has established and aligned for you, and knowing that purpose in
knowing that destiny, and knowing what God is taking you, you will
know you will no longer play around with your destiny anymore, but
you'll see the importance of your destiny.

Your importance of moving forward. Your portents of going
forward, and the importance of your life as it pertains to God doing it
in this time and season that you begin to walk it out, that you begin to
live it out, and that you begin to birth it out in this season. The one
thing that I like about purpose, is that sometimes we may find
ourselves becoming lost in our purpose. But when you grab hold to
God and he grabs hold to you, you find that your purpose is no longer

lost, and that you are not lost in it, but rather you are walking in your purpose, you're walking in you're calling, you're walking and all that God has ordained for your life, and you're walking in that which God has given for you to do when you really know what God has called you to do.

No one can deter you from it because you are fixated on completing that purpose. When you understand that God have called you, that he has chosen you, that he has ordained you that he has handpicked you that he has highlighted you for such a time as is that you begin to walk in that what he has called you to do that you begin to live out your purpose in the earth in the acceleration process, as you are soaring as you are gliding as you are on the airplane of your life, you have to understand that in the acceleration process, you cannot get lost in your purpose, you cannot get lost in your destiny, you cannot get lost in what you're called to do. But you must understand and recognize that in your purpose is the fulfillment of your destiny being established for such a time as this.

You must keep accountability. India celebration process. You must have people around you that help you, your accountability circle is ones that help push you. They pray for you, they're there for you. And they're helping you to push out you and your destiny. In your accountability team is should one that consists of men or women that help you to be all that you need to be in God and more. but they should also hold you accountable to live in a life that represents God, hold you accountable to integrity, hold you accountable to excellence, hold you accountable to your relationships, hold you accountable to you keeping your word hold you accountable to you doing what you're supposed to do.

I pray that in your accountability circle that each person holds you accountable to live in your life that you have been called by God to live and hold you accountable to doing all that you have been chosen by God to do so your circle, should be aligned with people that have your vision that should be aligned with people that understand your purpose should be aligned with people that understand where you are going and understand the importance of why you are going and help keep you accountable to getting there. I don't know about you, but I want to circle of accountability that we're flying on the plane together, that our vision aligns that our purpose aligns that our destiny is aligned.

And we understand the importance of helping one another to get where we're going, that's ever so important that we as sons and daughters of God, understand the importance of accountability and holding each other accountable. I have accountability in my life, even now. And it helps me to grow. It helps me to develop. It helps me to be better, and it helps me to walk and all that God has called me to do another part of the acceleration process is to move with the movers and shakers in your life. I don't know about you, but I have some great movers and shakers in my life that are also my accountability partners, and they helped me to grow. They helped me to develop.

They helped me to grow stronger and God in these movers and shakers are not stagnant, they're on the acceleration plane with me. They're soaring high with me in the air. They're Eagles that soaring and reaching for goals that going after their dreams they're going after all that God has for them in their lives. They're going after all that God has ordained for them, they're not being in a place of mediocrity. They're not in a place of stagnancy but however they are movers and shakers that are living out their lives as God has intended. We should be. As such, we should live our lives with the movers and shakers that are moving and our destiny is moving in our purpose, moving in our calling movie and all that God has called us to do, moving and shaking us to make history for God, that as we accelerate, we shall be the movers and shakers as we accelerate, we shall move into our destiny, as we accelerate, we shall move into the promises of that which God have a line for our lives. And the last part of the acceleration process is to keep us circle that pushes you to be even greater.

So now that you have your accountability, and you have your movers and shakers. Now you're going to have a circle that pushes you to be even greater that as you are soaring as you are advancing as you are moving in the kingdom of God, you know now that your prayer life helps you. Your facet life keeps you hearing God, or sustains you, your purpose aligns you and your destiny now connects you your accountability centers you and the movers and shakers that push you are pushing you forward that you may accelerate even higher than the things of God, that you will not be in a place of non-movement, but you'll be in a place of motion that you'll be in a place of greater that you reach your greater and this time in your life that you reach the greater that God has ordained for you, that you reach the greater that he has a line for you that the greater is coming, the greater is here, the greater is upon us.

This is the acceleration process that you saw higher and God, that you reach deeper and all that God intended for you, that you go even higher than you could ever have imagined. This is a time that you shall have salary. This is a time that you shall move forward. This is a time that the acceleration shall begin to happen in your life. There's a limping advancement.

There's a kingdom of God happening for your time in your life that you are moving, and the promises of which God has aligned, that you are moving and all that He has given unto you. It's time to accelerate. No longer will you sit and watch as others move. But you'll move to, because you're getting ready to ascend to higher and God than you can ever have imagined doors that was once closed will now be opened. You shall experience a move of God in your life in a greater capacity than you can ever have imagined. Once God moves in your life.

Watch God open doors. Once God begins to pour into you Even now, embrace all that God has given unto you on this great day, that as you continue reading these pages that you may know and understand that there is an acceleration process that God has given for your life. That as you begin to step into it. As you are sowing on your airplane of life that you reach your final destiny and Jesus in understanding the importance of all that God has given them to you and more.

There is this plane called life does this plane called destiny. Does the plane called acceleration, think God has you on it now? As you ascend higher as you go deeper and the things of God. May you know and remember how important you are to God and how important your life is to him. So, as you reach the higher heights in a deeper debt somewhere God is taking you begin to soar into the promises, for your life begins to soul. Begin to soar. It is your appointed and set time in God to soar.

Chapter Nine

Prepare for Landing/ Take the Quantum Leap

The most celebrated moments for some come when there is a completion of several assignments or activities over a period in one's life. The preparation of landing is the same. The Captain which is our Lord and Savior makes sure that we are prepared for the landing by ensuring that the flight crew that he has chosen goes around and makes sure that we are safe and that we are prepared for the landing that is getting ready to take place.

There is a quantum leap that occurs when the landing is taking places that bypasses the dichotomy of time and leaps forward unto an even greater measure of the moment. In a most recent article cited by author Andrew Jaffe from nature.com in 2018 he asserts as follows, "According to theoretical physicist Carlo Rovelli, time is an illusion: our naive perception of its flow doesn't correspond to physical reality. Indeed, as Rovelli argues in *The Order of Time*, much more is illusory, including Isaac Newton's picture of a universally ticking clock. Even Albert Einstein's relativistic space-time — an elastic manifold that contorts so that local times differ depending on one's relative speed or proximity to a mass — is just an effective simplification." (www.nature.com, 2018)

According to dictionary.com a quantum leap is defined as follows, "a huge, often sudden, increase or advance in something." As we see this now as the forward motion of continual movement that God wants to have for our lives, we must move forward in all that God has ordained for us to do in life. The motion of movement that God has for us now is one that is rather swift in that what would have taken years to manifest or come into fruition we are able to receive it in days and weeks. There has arisen a quantum leap in our lives to push and propel us forth swiftly into all that God has aligned for our lives as kingdom citizens.

We have divine access and privileges to all that he has unlocked for us and it is going to happen instantly for some and weeks for others. Merriam Webster defines a quantum leap as follows, 'an abrupt change, sudden increase, or dramatic advance. Note: Quantum leap is rarely used in scientific contexts, but it originated as a synonym of quantum jump, which describes an abrupt transition (as of an electron, an atom, or a molecule) from one discrete energy state to another.

The quantum leap represents the revelation that God has given unto us in the spirit. It indicates the revelation and the knowledge that God has given to us through the Holy Spirit which is our divine paraclete. In Revelation 3:20 it says, "Here I am! I stand at the door and knock. If anyone hears my voice and opens the door, I will come in and eat with them, and they with me." God is waiting for us to ascend and to come up higher in Him. He wants to open doors for us and extend to us mysteries and unlock Heaven and realms on our behalf.

In Revelations 19:11 it says, "I saw heaven standing open and there before me was a white horse, whose rider is called Faithful and True. With justice he judges and makes war." God is ascending us into higher places in Him and as we ascend and have a desire to go even deeper and experience the true revelation that he has for our lives we can then experience an even greater relationship with God and advance into all that he wants in our lives. In 1 Corinthians 4:1 it says, "This, then, is how you ought to regard us: as servants of Christ and as those entrusted with the mysteries God has revealed." In Luke 8:10 it says, "He said, "The knowledge of the secrets of the kingdom of God has been given to you, but to others I speak in parables, so that, "though seeing, they may not see; though hearing, they may not understand." Also, in Matthew 13:11 it says, "He replied, "The knowledge of the secrets of the kingdom of heaven has been given to you, but not to them."

There is coming unto our lives as we continue to advance in God more opportunities to experience the revelation and movement of God in our lives. The advancement of more wisdom and understanding as well as more insight and revelation.

Chapter Ten

Arrival/ Final Destination

Now that we have properly ascended and now descended safely the last and final process of acceleration is making it to our last and final destination. There are many that will make it to their final destinations in an accelerated time because they have discovered their purpose in life, and they have followed through on and completed it.

The most beautiful thing in the world that one can discover is their purpose and then the even greater prolusion of this is knowing what we have been called to do, completing it and then helping others to do the same. We are not here for just happenstance or chance, but God has called, and he has chosen us with a purpose in the earth that is to be fulfilled. When we reach our final destination from the arrival of our planes of life we can then assemble and then prepare for the legacy of the next generation that is coming after us to follow.

There is so much power in leaving a legacy that is going to make a true impact on the world leading up to our name with God being the leading name of it all. The way we begin and finish our lives is so important. From now and until we take our last breath there is such an acceleration that will occur and happen over the course of time. It is up to us to capture the moment and to embrace the power of the accelerated path that God has given to us. Some will look at the path and reason within themselves to believe that it is too fast, and that life is to be lived at a slower pace so out of fear they then talk themselves out of the good that God is bringing into their lives. Then there are some who reach the destination only to find out that it was everything that they could have imagined and more. While there are others who want to hide and forget about life by drowning themselves with loads of extra things to do to consume their time of fulfilling their destiny.

It's time to advance in the kingdom of God and embrace all that God has given unto you and more. It's time to accelerate and propel with forward motion and movement in the spirit realm to receive all that God has ordained for your life and to obtain the beauty and mysteries that are yet to be unveiled on your behalf. May you embrace this time and moment as being your congratulatory moment of that you are now celebrated and cherished for all that you have been able to finally accomplish within this lifetime to leave a footprint and mark on this world. You have been hand-picked and as the elite of the elite to represent the warriors of the army of God and the royal priesthood of His divine kingdom.

About the Author

Dr. Monique Rodgers is an international best-selling author, Global speaker, ordained and licensed Prophetess, ordained minister, educator, entrepreneur and woman on the mission for God. Dr. Monique Rodgers completed her undergraduate at Oral Roberts University in Tulsa Oklahoma being a first-generation college student she didn't stop there she went on to obtain her Master of Science degree from Colorado Technical University where she maintained a

3.97 GPA. She then loved education so much that she went on to pursue her doctorate degree at Colorado Technical University in Global Leadership where she completed in 2017 top of her class. She has traveled to six nations: Africa, Mexico, Peru, Jamaica, Haiti and Thailand.

She is currently a writing coach for Beyond the Book Media. She is an International Distinguished Scholar. She is also a member of The International Society of Female Professionals. She is the founder of Repairing the World Through the Word Ministries in Raleigh North Carolina. Dr. Monique Rodgers has been a guest on radio programs such Rashael Speaks. She is tv host for The Healing Zone on WATCTOO. She also has a podcast called, The Love Walk.

She has a weekly broadcast called the Power Lunch Broadcast on The Glory Network every Friday. She also has a tv program that is aired called, The Miracle Zone on DCBN Broadcasting. Dr. Rodgers has also spoken on tv at God's Glory Radio TV Show. Dr. Rodgers always knew that God had called and gifted her to preach and to write. When she was seven years old, she hands wrote books and sold them for quarter to her friends. She always knew that she was destined to be a scribe and a writer for God's glory. Her writing has been truly that a gift comes easier for her than most to complete. She has self-published 12 books. Her first book was a collection of poems called Poems of Inspiration. Her next book was called Hello! My name is Millennial, following that she wrote, A More Simple Life, A Majestical Land of Twinville, Picking up the Pieces, Falling in Love with Jesus and many more.

Her newest book called Accelerate which you are now holding in your hand and another called I am Black History will be released at the same time. Dr. Rodgers is also a vegan and advocates when she can for heath events. She is also a certified life coach, vegan nutrition health coach and a mentor to many. Her passion is for helping the lost, hurt and the broken for Jesus. She has studied at the Black Business School and preparing to work on her certification in Business Analytics at Harvard Business School online. She aspires to leave a legacy to her family. Dr. Rodgers is a survivor she has overcame abuse, eating disorders, and homelessness. She aspires to write one hundred books.

Notes/Reflections

If this book has changed your life email the author today at drmoniquerodgers@gmail.com